Velociraptor

BY BARBARA ALPERT

Amicus High Interest is published by Amicus
P.O. Box 1329, Mankato, MN 56002
www.amicuspublishing.us

Library of Congress Cataloging-in-Publication Data
Alpert, Barbara.
 Velociraptor / by Barbara Alpert.
    p. cm. -- (Digging for dinosaurs)
 Summary: "Describes how the Velociraptor was discovered,
how paleontologists study its bones, and what the fossil
evidence tells us about the behavior of this small, speedy
meat-eating dinosaur"-- Provided by publisher.
 Includes bibliographical references and index.
 ISBN 978-1-60753-370-2 (library binding) -- ISBN 978-1-
60753-418-1 (ebook)
 1. Velociraptor--Juvenile literature. I. Title.
 QE862.S3A4355 2014
 567.912--dc23

                              2013001229

Editor   Rebecca Glaser
Series Designer   Kathleen Petelinsek
Page Production   Red Line Editorial, Inc.

Photo Credits
Dreamstime, cover; De Agostini/Getty Images, 4, 10;
Michael Rosskothen/Shutterstock Images, 7; Photos 12/
Alamy, 8; Mark Hallett Paleoart/Getty Images, 13; Chris
George/Alamy, 14; EmmePi Images/Alamy, 17; J. Lekavicius/
Shutterstock Images, 18; Galyna Andrushko/Shutterstock
Images, 21; Ted S. Warren/AP Images, 22; Michael
Rosskothen/123RF, 25, 29; Mick Ellison/American Museum
of Natural History/AP Images, 26

Printed in the United States of America at Corporate Graphics
in North Mankato, Minnesota.
5-2013 / PO 1148
10 9 8 7 6 5 4 3 2 1

Table of Contents

The **Protoceratops** and the
Velociraptor were enemies.

 How fast was Velociraptor?

What is a Velociraptor?

A Velociraptor hid. The dinosaur stood on two legs. It saw a Protoceratops munching on leaves. The Velociraptor was hungry, too. It was small and quick. It was much faster than the bigger dinosaur. It ran. Then it chomped on the Protoceratops's leg, biting hard with its sharp teeth.

Scientists think it could run up to 40 miles (64 km) per hour.

Protoceratops tried to run or shake it off. But the Velociraptor held on. Its long, curved back claw cut into the dinosaur's skin. Who would win? Other Velociraptors joined in too. Some bit the tail. Others climbed up its back. The small, fierce animals worked as a group. They killed the much bigger dinosaur. Time to eat!

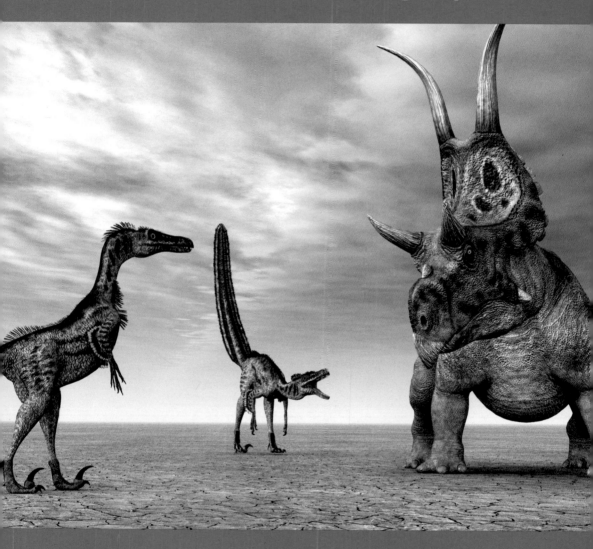

Roy Chapman Andrews and his team found bones in Mongolia.

 Why choose the name "speedy thief"?

The Discovery of Velociraptor

In the 1920s, Roy Chapman Andrews took a crew to explore Mongolia. His men dug up many dinosaur bones. In 1923, his team found a crushed skull. They also found a large, sharp claw. It was a new dinosaur! It was named Velociraptor. This means "speedy thief."

Because of its small size. Scientists thought it would have grabbed food and run away.

Velociraptor had a large skull
with lots of sharp teeth.

 What else can the skull tell us?

Velociraptor had a long skull. It had space for a big brain. At least, it was big compared to the size of its body. So it must have been smarter than other dinosaurs of its time.

Velociraptor was built to catch **prey**. Its mouth was full of pointed teeth. The giant toe claw was curved. It could cut open an animal's skin.

A The eyeholes are large. Velociraptor had eyes on the sides of its head, like a bird. It likely had very good eyesight.

In 1971, scientists from China and Poland made an amazing discovery. They dug up a whole Velociraptor. It was fighting when it died. Its big toe claw cut into the neck of a Protoceratops. The Protoceratops had one of the Velociraptor's arms in its jaws. Scientists had guessed how the Velociraptor used its claws. Now there was proof.

 How big was Velociraptor?

A Protoceratops was much heavier than a Velociraptor.

A **Fossils** show it was 5 to 6 feet (1.5 to 2 m) long. It was about 3 feet (1 m) tall.

The leg bones of this dinosaur
show that it could run fast.

Fossil Clues

The fossil **site** in Mongolia is called the "Flaming Cliffs." It has many Velociraptor bones. Most were found in the past 40 years. Each new fossil gives clues to the life of this dinosaur. Leg bones show it might have run as fast as a horse. Claws on hands and feet could help it climb tall dinosaurs. It may have done this to attack.

Velociraptor had three claws on each hand. It had four on each back foot. The front claws grabbed its prey. Its sharp back claws did the killing. Velociraptor was often smaller than its prey. It would have been hard to kill a big animal. So some scientists think it held its prey and started eating it before it was dead. Eagles and hawks do this, too.

 Did Velociraptor always kill for food?

Fossils show Velociraptor had three fingers.

 We don't know for sure. It could have been both a **predator** and a **scavenger**. If it found food on the ground, it likely ate it.

The Flaming Cliffs hold many bones. But how are they sorted out? **Paleontologists** make maps. They keep track of where dinosaur bones are found. Scientists study the maps. They have seen that many Velociraptor bones were dug up near other Velociraptors. This may mean they hunted and lived in packs.

The Flaming Cliffs is a fossil site in Asia.

Scientists studied the soil where the fossils were found. They think Velociraptors died in sand storms. The dinosaurs were buried alive in a sand slide. A huge amount of sand slid down a hill like an avalanche. Mongolia is hot and dry. That kept the fossils in good condition.

Fossils have stayed in good condition in the Gobi desert.

Hollow bones made
raptors light and fast.

 What else do raptors have in common?

A Family of Raptors

The Velociraptor had many relatives. Some were much bigger, like the Utahraptor. The raptors were all meat-eating dinosaurs that moved fast. They all ran on two legs. All had a powerful curved claw. Most were smarter than big dinosaurs. They all had hollow bones, like birds.

 They laid eggs. Fossil raptor eggs were found in Montana.

Deinonychus is also a raptor. Its bones have been found in the United States. It was bigger than Velociraptor. But its tracks look close to the same. Scientists found tracks that looked like footprints of Deinonychus. Six of them moved together. The **trackways** give more proof that raptors lived in groups.

Deinonychus was larger than Velociraptor.

This Velociraptor arm bone shows bumps where feathers attached.

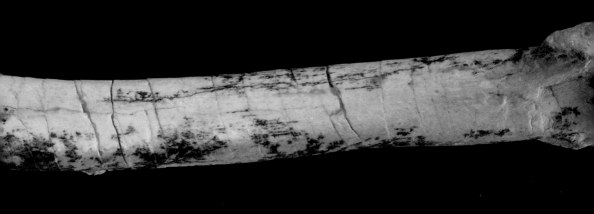

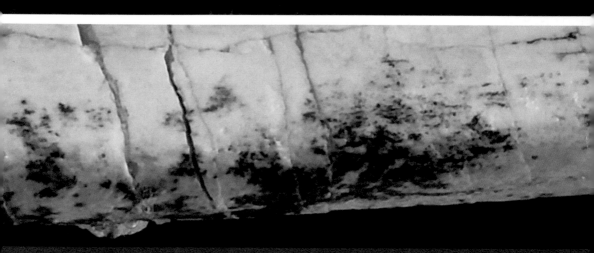

 **Q** If Velociraptor had feathers, could it fly?

Velociraptor Today

In 2007, scientists found new clues. They studied a Velociraptor arm bone. It had **quill knobs**! Birds have these bumps on their wings where the feathers connect. Quill knobs prove that Velociraptor had feathers on its arms. Many scientists think birds are related to dinosaurs. This discovery gave more proof to that idea.

 Probably not. Its arms were too small for the size of its body to be able to fly.

In 2010, scientists in China dug up more Velociraptor bones. Again, they were next to a Protoceratops. Bite marks were seen on the head of Protoceratops. Scientists think Velociraptor ate it, but did not kill it. It was already dead. What else we will learn about this speedy thief?

Velociraptor means "speedy thief."

Glossary

fossil The remains of a plant or animal of a past age preserved in earth or rock.

paleontologist A scientist who studies fossils.

predator An animal that hunts other animals for food.

prey An animal eaten by other animals.

quill knob A bump where feathers attach to bones.

scavenger An animal that eats leftovers when it finds them on the ground.

site A place where something happens or where something is found.

trackway A series of fossil footprints.

Read More

Dodson, Peter. *Velociraptor Up Close: Swift Dinosaur.* Berkeley Heights, N.J.: Enslow Publishers, 2011.

Mara, Wil. *Velociraptor.* Rookie Read-About-Dinosaurs. New York: Children's Press, 2012.

Riggs, Kate. *Velociraptor.* When Dinosaurs Lived. Mankato, Minn.: Creative Paperbacks, 2012.

Websites

Velociraptor Facts and Pictures—National Geographic Kids
http://kids.nationalgeographic.com/kids/animals/creaturefeature/velociraptor-mongoliensis/

Velociraptor—thedinosaurs.org
http://www.thedinosaurs.org/dinosaurs/velociraptor.aspx

Velociraptor—Enchanted Learning
http://www.enchantedlearning.com/subjects/dinosaurs/dinos/Velociraptor.shtml

Index

About the Author

Barbara Alpert has written more than 20 children's books and many books for adults. She lives in New York City, where she works as an editor. She loves to travel and has collected fossils in New York, New Jersey, Montana, and Pennsylvania.